# You Are Loved: Letters from Strangers Who Love You

*You Are Loved*

All Rights Reserved.
Easy Publishing Company
Salt Lake City, Utah 84119
http://www.easypublishingcompany.com
contact@easypublishingcompany.com

ISBN-13: 978-0692281895
ISBN-10: 0692281894

First Edition: September 2014
Printed in the United States of America

This book is dedicated to Angela Fries, a beautiful young woman who left us too soon.

# Introduction

When I was sixteen years old, I was having a very difficult time in my life. I was kicked out of my house and had to live with "friends". I dropped out of school so that I could work enough to buy food. I was being abused verbally, physically, and emotionally by several people in my life. I started counting days, then weeks, and then months since someone had said something nice to me.

I would have given anything to hear a complement. Pretty soon, I started believing all of the crappy things that were being said to me and about me. There were two people in my life at this time that asked me every day why I didn't just kill myself. I started wondering the same thing.

I started to think about how I would kill myself. I didn't want to do anything that would leave a mess or make anyone else hate me. I wished that I could afford a beautiful dress that I could wear when I died. That way, when I was found, people would say something nice about me. I finally decided that I would just swim as far as I could out into the ocean at night.

As I was getting ready to carry out this plan, I felt like I was at the mercy of the world. I lost all hope. I couldn't feel joy. I didn't have any emotions. One night, I was waiting the table of a middle-aged woman. She ordered a coffee, but didn't say anything else to me. Even without conversation, I felt some sort of connection to her. When I looked into her eyes, I didn't feel like I needed to immediately look away. I didn't feel judged.

When she left, I went to clean up her table. She left me a note written on a napkin that read, "I can tell that you are a special person. Thank you for being a part of my life." Before I even finished reading this note, I was sobbing uncontrollably. All I needed was for someone to appreciate some part of me. I just needed to hear something positive about myself. It was like I had won the lottery. Needless to say, I didn't kill myself and I quickly turned my life around.

Because of this experience, I have decided to publish a collection of letters from people all across the world who love you. True, they may not have met you, but that didn't stop them from writing you a letter to tell you that they love you. Life is hard. Life is tough. Life isn't fair. Sometimes life will bring you down to the lowest levels that you could possibly bear. But all of us are here to tell you that it will get better. The best part about being in your lowest of lows is that it's only up from here. Sometimes you will feel like you are all alone. But you aren't alone. We are here with you. We love you. We know your value. We know your worth. You are important. You are needed.

You are Loved.

**NOTE:** The letters that follow have been submitted by many people located across the globe. For several of them, their first language isn't English. Most of the others aren't full time English professors. That being said, this book has gone through a thorough editing process, but we have opted to try and leave most of the entries with minimal changes. Please forgive any slightly confusing sentences and enjoy the spirit of the book.

# A Collection of Letters from People who Love You:

# 1

Hello friend, welcome (back) to the party! "What party?" you might ask, and your right: It might not seem to be a very nice party or a party at all.

Most of us think so when we just come in, wet from the rain, glasses foggy from the heat, pushed aside by others leaving early or arriving late. Some of us only start to realize what it is, when they awake with a severe hangover. But believe me, in some weird way it's a party.

To be honest: it's a total mess. The host is nowhere to be found, most of the guests are drunk, stupid, ugly, rude or all of that combined and the music is much too loud. Most of the time, it's impossible to have a meaningful conversation.

But there's more to this party than the sweaty dancers in the living room, the networkers in the hallway, the hipsters in the kitchen and all the other creepy people. So feel at home and have a look. I promise there is some interesting stuff to see and some very nice people to meet. People just like you, in fact.

I for example like the attic. All those dusty chests and wardrobes! And if you're done looking for pirate treasures and magical lands you can climb on the roof and have a look at the city. It's so beautiful from up there and maybe you spot a place, you want to visit.

When I first came to the party I was terrified. I wondered if the bouncer had some cruel joke at my expense, when he let me in. Everything I did felt wrong. I wore the wrong clothes. I didn't belong here. I didn't know anybody. I didn't even speak the language!

But the food was OK, the music good (you know, in my days they still knew how to play real music) and there was a small library down the hallway. And so I met my first few friends. Well, not real friends you might argue since all of them were long dead or didn't even exist outside of their books. But I don't care, because I like them anyway and I think they like me, too.

After a while others joined me in the library or invited me to different places in the house: The gym, the cinema, even the secret basement. I watched what they did, what they liked and I learned from them.

At first I didn't say much. I smiled shyly. Sometimes I recommended a good book. But little by little I also learned to ask. Did you know, that you can ask for almost anything and that ,no' isn't the final answer but an invitation?

So I'm asking you to stay a little bit longer and maybe tell me your story. Grab one of those sandwiches (You have to try one of those, they are delicious!), let me get you a cold milkshake or a hot chocolate and then let's see, if we can learn something from one another.

Thanks for staying. The party is so much better, because you are here. And hey, you know what? Let's find some more friends and start our own party!

Cheers,

Sebastian

# 2

"Hello stranger! I know how it feels to have no hope left, when life looks like there is no point in going on. I have been there many times. This is the time when I go for a walk and look at nature around me: the trees, the animals, the waves, the sun, the moon and many stars at night. Then I am reminded that there is a creator out there who loves me, whose wisdom surpasses mine. I might not understand it. I might not see it in the moment but I am certain I am not alone in my hour of need. And then I pray that he would show me my purpose in life. And he answers. Not by giving me the full plan but by showing me the next small step. And as I take the next small step my hope returns and new opportunities are coming my way. "

Kind regards,

Mark

# 3

Being happy is sometimes something that's hard to do. You can't just look up "how to be happy" online or in a book. But I think my favorite explanation on how to be happy came from a child. All he said was "Don't think bad thoughts." Something that probably sounds so simply yet extremely difficult all at the same time coming from a child. But I think it's probably the best advice someone could ever give you.

-Ashley Carey

# 4

To Whomever You May Be:

As a writer and child sexual abuse survivor who has written about the horror of child sexual abuse from a child's perspective, I'm writing now to offer a message of hope.

There were times in my adult life that felt every bit as dark as the episodes of my childhood abuse, and during some of those times the lure of suicide as a "way out" presented itself with compelling force.

But every one of those times I made the decision to live, and—however haltingly, however imperfectly—to try to heal the wounds of my childhood. And what always served to sustain me was the taking of the action—an action at once intellectual and emotional—of giving myself permission to love and accept myself precisely as I was at those darkest moments. Yes, to accept every single part of myself, including the part of me that so desperately wanted a "way out" of my then current circumstances—a desire which, after all, is perfectly reasonable when one is in despair, the chief question being the method one chooses for pursuing one's way out, whether that method will or will not involve a continued commitment to life and living.

My deep hope, then, is that if you now or ever find yourself in such a state of utter darkness you will give yourself permission—even if no one else is giving it—to love yourself exactly as you are, since self-acceptance, in my experience, has proven to be the fundamental basis of any lasting positive change. Regardless of how others may want you to be; regardless, even, of others' hatred, love yourself as you are, for by doing so, you'll enable yourself to become, more and more, the person you want to be.

With Love,

John Brooks

Writer & Child Sexual Abuse Survivor

Author of Preludes, an extended short story chronicling the experiences of a nine-year-old boy as he struggles to survive sexual abuse by his father in a middle class American family

johnbrookswriting.com

# 5

You will be missed

And leave a hole in people's hearts

Where you once stood

If you were to go away


So lean on these people

With your fears

Your problems concerns

And together step into another day


-Jon Stroh

# 6

You are loved,

I have been where you are now. Without hope. No way out. Feeling that everyone would be better off if you were gone.

I have been where you are now. Thousands of plans running through my head. Wading through each day seeing the worst batter me again.

I have been where you are now. I hear only criticism and condemnation. Nothing I do is right or makes things right.

I have been where you are now. No one is listening to my pain. Will they listen when I can't speak my heart.

I have been where you are now. Crying over someone loved that I will never see again. How could anyone else understand?

I have been where you are now. What stayed my hand when things were darkest and I was so ready to embrace the long night? Was it someone smiling and inviting me to play a game? Was it a little girl smiling at me and giving me hugs? Was it falling down wet stone steps and being driven to my knees when I decided this was the day?

It was all of these. The little things of life. Pebbles and stones that showed the ripples of our actions touching all shores.

I have been where your family, friends, and fellow workers will be asking "Why"?

I have felt the guilt of the living asking "Why"?

I have felt the pain of those left behind asking "Why"?

I have felt the agony those left behind saying "if only..."

Things will not change if you are dead. Who will you not be there for if you gone?

Will someone else die without your smile? Will someone else never find love? Who will you be the example for?

You are loved; Let me see your smile!

"Don"

Survivor of many things of the Roller Coaster of Life

Survivor of an Employee's Suicide

To My Dearest Friend-

I have seen you when you thought you were unnoticed. I listened when you spoke. I found joy in your laughter and I have even felt the tears as you have cried. Those moments when the pain was hardest were the moments when I was reaching out to you. I have seen you when you felt invisible. I have wished happiness would fill your soul and never leave. You are my friend. You are my sister. You are my brother. You are the person I smile at as we pass each other on the road. I dream of your smile even when you cannot find the strength to make it yourself. When the sun lights on your skin I am within it. I am the beauty that exists even when you can no longer see it. I am the wind daring to run through your hair if only for a second. I long to show you the beauty that you truly are.

When the day sets into the evening and the moon is all that can be seen, you are the Sun to me. You are surrounded by love. Your skin is basking in it. Your breath is taking it in. Your feet are walking beside it. Your hands are brushing it aside. There is an abundance of love all around you. I want you to stop and look for it. Stop and pause within it. This world was made for you. The colors were chosen to bring beauty into your mind.

The scents were created to fill your lungs. The tastes were imagined to find you even in the simplest of tasks. All of this was made with exquisite care and yet it still pales in comparison to the beauty that is you. Have you seen the world around you?

You are the reason love is possible. It was made by and for you. I have loved you. I have sent you love when you felt it no longer existed. Laughter and joy were created to express the simplest of pleasures. They were made so that we can share when our hearts are full. You are special. You have talents. You have a voice. You are everything and everyone. You are singular as well. I have spoken for you. I have spoken about you. I have spoken to you. I have known you and I have longed to know you. I have seen you when the pain tried to take you. I have seen your struggle. I have seen you fight even when you didn't think you were fighting. I have watched you persevere. I have seen the quiet calms and I have watched as wars were waged all within your delicate heart. You amaze me. You have overcome so much to be here today.

I know that you have felt loneliness. I know that you have questioned. I know that you have been pained by a sense that you are different. I want you to reach out. Touch the sky and look to the stars because I am looking with you. You are never alone. You are never truly alone. You are simply missing me and I am missing you. Together we are two. Together we are more than we were on our own. You are my life-saver. You are my reason for trying. You have shown me what strength is made of. You have proven that it can be done. You have allowed me to see more than what was meant for me. Your words have reached my ears. Your smile has touched my heart. Your life has lingered within my soul. You have given me hope. You have given me strength. You have given me you.

I will always be here with you. I will always reach out for you when you need a hand. I can never repay you for the gifts you have given me. I can never share the joy that your light brought into my life but I can always keep it within me. I can always do my best to share your gifts with others. You are an absolutely astonishing person. You are more than I could ever wish to be. You are more than even you see.

Look for me. I will be the one smiling at you.

From Me.

# 8

For anyone considering ending their life... you've missed something. No matter the situation, there is something you haven't thought of yet that will turn things around. No matter when or how many times... if this is your mind-set, your missed something. Think of what that is until you find it.

No matter how long that takes. It's there. You just haven't thought about it yet.

You will. I promise.

# 9

Love comes in different ways at different times but always when your soul is ready. Love yourself and everything will come in time.....

# 10

Dear One,

We are all parts of one big, beautiful, complex puzzle. Without all the pieces of the puzzle, the puzzle is not whole.

Your piece of the absolutely puzzle matters. YOU matter. Your part of the story matters. Your life matters. You are loved, important and needed, even if some days it doesn't feel like you are. Your love for others greatly matters. Your smile can make the day of someone who is feeling down. Your smile can light up a room. Your hug can make someone sad feel loved. All along the days of your life you have been a gift to others. Each day you have given joy to others even if you didn't realize it. Each day you have been a blessing on this earth.

As the movie "It's a Wonderful Life" shows, the world would be a much bleaker, sadder, lonelier place if you were not here. The world would be missing one of its brightest lights. We rejoice in your being. We rejoice in YOU! By your very presence on this planet, you make it a much better, happier place for all of us.

You ARE loved and cherished. The world's beautiful puzzle is not complete without you!

Sincerely,

One who knows and will always treasure you

**Who needs me? you ask me.**
Does a star need the sky?
Does a seed need sunlight to grow?
Does a baby need a mother to be born?
Does a fish need water to survive?
Do we need air to breath?
Do I need you here to love?
Do I need you here to hold?
Do I need you here to kiss?
Do I need you here to confide in?
**I truly need you!**
**The world needs you!**
**The planet needs you!**
You are more than just a body.
You are a friend and lover.
You are a daughter/son/mother/father.
You are a student of life.
You are a teacher to others.
You are a ray of sunshine to others in crisis.
You are an example of strength and courage.
You are an example of compassion and kindness.
You an example of unconditional love and giving.
You are an example of all that is good in this world.
You are needed by more people than you will ever be able
to count!
You are absolutely, positively needed on this earth
and **you are loved!**

-Freeda Lapos Babson

# 12

You are loved with a love that is patient with you. Patient with the discouraging loops that are playing in your head right now. Patient with you, now in your misery, not in a hurry with you. Never annoyed that you are not getting better fast enough. You are loved right now, it's not a love that will release only to you when you get back to health.

You are loved with a kind love. It will never say horrible things to you. It does not delight in seeing any part of you die, not one little weakness, not one little flaw. Because there is no flaw in you.

You are loved with a love that is for you. For your soul and for your benefit. It does not feel threatened by your weirdness, it does not need to feel better or smarter or stronger than you. You are loved by someone who is for you, not against you.

You are loved with a love that does not insist that you turn your life around or obey or do what is right. It will not be irritable or resentful that you aren't changing enough or demonstrating enough sorriness or any other act of control. You are loved with full freedom to walk your own path as you will, at your pace and in your cadence.

Don't think for a moment that when bad things happen to you, this love abandons you to your misery. It does not celebrate or get smug, or say, "karma is a bitch." In fact, it celebrates when you can live more honestly, it congratulates you when you come out with the truth about who you are, and no matter what happens as a result of your honesty, it goes through the fire by your side, telling you "you did a good thing."

You are loved with a love that will never wear out, it is stronger than death and more enduring than the grave. You are loved when you wake and when you sleep, when you go out and when you come home, when you have a good day and when you have a bad one. You are loved when you try, and loved when you fail to try.

1 Corinthians 13:4-7 "Love is patient and kind; love does not envy or boast; it is not arrogant or rude. It does not insist on its own way; it is not irritable or resentful; it does not rejoice at wrongdoing, but rejoices with the truth. Love bears all things, believes all things, hopes all things, endures all things."

# 13

Dear Ones: in writing this letter I tried to come up with a way to define what it is to be loved. It wasn't until I started to think about it that I realized what a challenge I had facing me! We know ourselves what it is to love; we know the warm feeling it gives us and the joy it brings to our lives. But who can really define what it is to be loved? To me, it is life's greatest gift. To know we are loved by others, gives us meaning and purpose in a world that is often filled with doubt and confusion. To be loved assures that we matter, we belong, and we return happiness just by being the person we are. I think L. Frank Baum summed it up best in his classic book The Wonderful Wizard of Oz: "A heart is not judged by how much you love; but by how much you are loved by others."

Chris Davis

# 14

Dear Loved Ones:

You are Loved, and you are not alone. Everyone at some point in their lives have been through some rough patches. It is through the love of family and friends, or the kindness of strangers that can pull you through. The love and support is there, you just need to grab it and embrace it.

You are Loved, and you are not alone. You may feel like you are alone, but you are not. There are so many people that feel the same way you do. Seek out a support group and help each other. Helping others gives you reasons for giving and receiving love.

You are Loved, and you are not alone. Talk with your family and friends. They cannot help you if you do not seek out help from them. They will be supportive and understanding. But you need to communicate and give them a chance to prove it to you.

You are Loved, Love yourself and love and accept love from those around you. You are not alone.

Sharon Davis

# 15

Dear Reader,

It is difficult to know what to say to someone that is contemplating ending their life. It is hard to believe this is possible when at the same time others would give anything for one more minute on this earth. I wish I knew the answer and I'm sure many others do as well. I've been in dark places at times in my life as I believe most people have at one time or another. Every individual's circumstances are unique; however they share a common ground in that most people just want the pain to end. I have the great fortune to have faith in God, a wonderfully supportive and loving family, and kind friends. Therefore, I am lucky to have had a kind shoulder or two to lean on when needed. Everyone has different reasons to sink into a depression where suicide seems to be the only way out, and I can understand that. I feel that hopelessness is one of, if not the worst emotion to contend with. Second to that, I believe is betrayal.

I think that the loss of love whether from an affair, divorce, death, or a general falling-out is one of the largest contributors to feelings of hopelessness. It can be hard to find the light when you are amongst the darkness. In times when I have dealt with that great, dark enemy I have conquered it in various ways; talking to someone ~ anyone willing to listen, taking things one day at a time and trying to focus on getting through each day, reading ~ as this is the best form of escapism, writing poetry, a journal, or a letter explaining your feelings (even if it isn't sent), giving to and helping others ~ as this shifts the focus of your problems to those of other people, praying, reading the Bible, finding your passion through hobbies and the arts, remembering that your situation may be small in comparison to what others are going through (although that doesn't mean your situation is less important), and patience in letting time help lessen the pain. Sometimes I find that I feel better when I put my feelings in verse, as I have below.

## Let Your Life

The light had left the room
The flowers were no longer in bloom
And I wondered to myself
Is this it, or is there something else

I felt there was no way out
For no one had heard me shout
From the war going on in my mind
To this, all others were blind

There is pain in losing all hope
And death seems the way to cope
Yet deep in my soul there's a spark
That will lead me out of this dark

This spark fans the flames of light
My only choice now is to fight
For this life that was given me
To show others how dark it can be

Don't give up, don't give in, don't let go
I know for He told me so
As He walks along my side
I see that in my pain, I must bide

Easy my life is not
However, many others have already fought
So I could choose to have this life
Despite my heartache and my strife

If death was truly the key
Then this world would no longer be
Filled with those who forever stand strong
Against the end, for they know they belong

Stand up, walk forward, carry on
Seek comfort in showing others the dawn
That breaks on the face of the brave

So let your life be the one that you save

Please remember that you are never alone in this life. It may seem so at times, but God is there, watching over you and knowing how your heart feels. There is beauty in faith, in that it takes courage to believe that God is there and all hope is not lost. Remember and repeat to yourself, "never give up!" Seek help and comfort in others, for there are those that do love you. As I firmly believe, "In God I know I've won!"

With Love,
Fay Hullinger Hill
Carlton, Minnesota

# 16

This letter goes to all the people who have close ones who suffer from depression.

A little story about myself: There is a person I really like. This person suffers or suffered from depression. There were the funny times and we could laugh and be happy together.

But there also were the bad times where she was in a down. These times were the hardest. First I wanted to help her with motivating her to go outside or to watch a film or just anything that would make her feel better. But she never wanted to do anything. This went on for the first few weeks that we knew each other. The more downs that came the more I started getting angry. Not angry at her. Angry at me. Why wasn't I able to help her. I tried everything but nothing did help. I began feeling down myself. And with feeling down I realized you don't want to talk if you are down, you don't want to go outside, you don't want to do anything. Luckily she helped me through these down times even if she wasn't in the best mood.

Slowly, I began to realize how I could help. From then on, if she was down I was there. Maybe hugged her or sat beside her. I did not talk but if she wanted to talk I listened to her and slowly the "uptimes" began to outweigh the downtimes. Today there are rarely any real downs. And if they occur we are comforting each other. And we both know it will get better.

What I want to say with this story is that you can't do anything against it immediately. It's a slow process. All you can do is giving the feeling of safety and comfort. And slowly they will realize that they are loved. That they are safe. Don't let it pull you down too deep. You also need to think about yourself. If you are feeling depressed to consider getting some professional help before it's too late.

Last, but not least I want to perform a little magic trick. This letter has eyes did you know? But you have to open them. Just say eyes and the letter will see you.

I didn't quite hear that was that "eyes"?

Ah now it works. You're really pretty, did you know that? If I wasn't a letter I would date you.

Regards

Philip Zimmermann

# 17

Depression is real but it's something we're not supposed to talk about, can't talk about, and don't talk about. But it's there. What you're feeling is real and it's true, and it sucks and it feels terrible and it makes you just want to give up. And that's exactly when you don't give up. You take one more breath and put one more foot in front of the other. Because no matter what you think in this moment, you are important and you do matter, you do mean something to someone even if it's just to yourself. You matter. So take that breath, smile for yourself, give yourself a little hug and keep going. For one more breath.

Julia Johnsen

# 18

Dear Reader,

I recently came across You Are Loved: A Campaign to Combat Suicide on the Kickstarter website. I have not yet received a copy of the book, but I found the description of the writing to very inspirational, and I look forward to receiving my own copy! Being a member of a demographic that is of high risk for committing suicide, and after attempting to take my own life in the past: I hope that this work can go on to save lives, and uplift the people's spirits with a new sense of hope!

Here is my story:

My name is Faith. I am a 19 year old transgender woman (MtF) living with my girlfriend (Michelle) in Seattle, Washington. It is not easy to be me. Sadly, 41% of all transgender people will, or already have attempted suicide at some point of their lives. Many are successful. Fortunately, I was not! My depression had gone far past what most people deal with; I began racking up suicide attempts, and I started to hurt myself at every chance I got. It went to the point where I didn't even want to exist!

There is a feeling of alienation that stems from being a person like myself. Aside from being born into the wrong body, so many of us are encouraged to go against the true nature of our personalities. It often causes a massive dysphonia, and hence our high rates of suicide. I however have found strength inside of myself, and I have used it to push on while simultaneously being true to myself.

Last year I came to Washington and I immediately started living full time as myself. Once I did this, everything brightened up; my whole life changed for the better! I began to feel compassion for everyone, including myself. I wanted to make everyone around me happy, and help anyone in need. I became an extrovert and I started to get to where I am now.

I am currently a student in college, a manager at my place of employment (yes, at 19!), and I even have an apartment in a nice location. I pass much of my free time by expressing myself with my art. I have supportive friends and family. I am completely turning my life around. I LOVE MY LIFE!

I cannot express how important it is to keep going forward and to live another day. Depression is only temporary, life as whole is much longer. Just stay alive and keep faith that everything will get better with time; keep persisting, be strong, and you will get through it. You'll be truly surprised just how wonderful life can get once you have passed this dark phase that was once in your life.

Much Love,

-Faith and Michelle

# 19

Has anyone told you today that you bring joy to the world? There is a beautiful Spirit living inside your quiet presence as you try to slip by unnoticed, your eyes downcast. You may not even be aware of that beautiful Spirit because all you have ever heard is awful things about yourself.

But you don't have to believe those people or the things they say and please try not to let their words get stuck inside your head on endless repeat. Find that beautiful Spirit deep inside yourself that you have hidden away and don't be afraid to acknowledge it, to embrace it, and to nurture it because you are a very special person and you are loved.

# 20

Dear Ones:

This is when we must see the error in our thinking. No problem is greater than we are. Look at the events that have occurred throughout history and you will see that time and time again humans have faced what appeared to be insurmountable odds but they were not defeated. They met the challenge head on and through their own determination, they conquered their problems.

You are an important part of the human family. Without you, our family would not be the same. We as members of the family are all necessary and we're all needed. When you wake up in the morning, say a prayer of thanks because you know that you are loved. At night before you go to sleep, remember that this was a day in which you were loved and tomorrow will be a brand new day of being loved.

There are many people in this big world but you are special. Why? Because you are you! Each of us brings something to the lives of others. When you do something nice for someone else, you have made a difference for that person. It could be as small as holding a door open for an elderly person or helping a small child to cross a busy street. It is not so much what you do, it is the love you send and the love you receive that matters.

Always remember, love is what binds us together as humans. You are here with us and you are loved!

Chris Davis

# 21

"The Service"

Shadorma  by

Sean Vessey 2014


Bright sunshine

Cheerless room asks "Why?"

A sister

A widow

Faithful wife follows her mate

Cheerless room asks "Why?"

## 22

"The Tears"

Shadorma  by

Sean Vessey 2014


I Live, Why?

Others I knew died

Tears don't End

Memories

Do I cry because I live?

For families' tears?

# 23

"Dark Ride"

Shadorma by

Sean Vessey 2014


Night time ride

Roll fast where few go

Is it time?

Call No Joy?

Cheerful Sun wakes my dream end

I wait for my ride

# 24

"You are loved"

Shadorma by

Sean Vessey 2014


You are loved

Lips' curves bring joy

Small ripples

Live today

Tomorrow waits for your smile

You are loved, please wait

# 25

Dear Reader,

I started cutting when I was 15. It was never about suicide, but about finding control in a situation I felt powerless in. My father was abusive, seeming to take joy in breaking me down emotionally and mentally as well as physically. It didn't take long for me to begin to crack. After a short while I couldn't feel anything but anger. I could feel the anger inside of me, it was a black ichor that took the place of my blood, and I had no way to get rid of it. That's when I discovered the razor.

I found control the first time I cut, and I relished it. The sharp pain cleared my head, and the anger seemed to drain out of me with every drop of blood. I fell in love with the blood, the way that the vibrant, rich, life-giving liquid would bead up from the slashes in my leg, only to slide down my skin.

I knew that people wouldn't understand the comfort I found while hurting myself, so I hid my canvas, wearing only long pants or skirts that would go down to my ankles. Even so, my mother and sister found out. Mom cried and my sister got angry, yelling at me for being so stupid, so weak. She threw away the razors and made me promise never to hurt myself again. Their reactions scared me. By the time I was 16, I had lost the part of me that could deal with strong emotions, sinking deeper and deeper into the apathy that depression brings. The vibrancy and strength of their anger, fear, and worry scared me. It made me want to cut more.

I would promise that I'd never cut again, and I'd be ashamed of my weakness and of the pain that I caused them. And I meant it. I meant it every time that I said I was done. But something would happen either at home or at school and I'd feel the need begin to rise. I'd start getting edgy, start dreaming of the color red, of the blood flowing across bared skin. I would break, pulling out another razorblade and drawing it across my skin. The first cut was always a relief, a soothing wave that would wash over my mind and body. I'd watch the blood trickle down and that blessed calm would take me again.

The guilt and shame would plague me afterwards, which would start the need building. After a while, every problem, every stressor brought the dreams and the whole world seemed to be washed in red. I didn't know what to do – my very escape became a prison.

Enter Jen.

To this day, I hold that Jen is one of the most beautiful girls I've ever met, inside and out. She had a light around her, and she was one of those people who could make you smile, just by smiling at you. Right when I thought that I couldn't hold everything together any longer, she invited me to spend the night at her house.

We spent hours watching anime and talking about any random things that popped into our minds. When we were changing for bed, Jen noticed my half-healed cuts and the scars from over a year of self-harm. When she reached out to pull the leg of my too-short and faded pajama pants up to my knee, I didn't stop her.

I was already preparing for the worst. I knew what would happen next: she would put on theatrics, yelling, crying, screaming, and telling me how what I was doing was wrong. She would make me promise never to do it again, and I'd have one more person to let down when I broke my promise. I pulled in on myself, staring into her face, waiting for the inevitable explosion. It never came.

Jen took a long time to look at the multitude of scars that crossed my leg, and all she said was, "Shibby design."

It was in that moment of acceptance and shared knowledge that I felt the piece of me that I thought had died, take root and begin to grow. She may not have seen me at my darkest, or my worst, but she had seen my private shame, my private salvation and did not flinch away. Jen didn't judge me, and even though I was flawed, she loved me. That knowledge gave me the strength to start looking outwards and that night, for the first time in a long time, I didn't dream in red.

And that brings us to you, dear Reader.

Sometimes when your world is breaking apart and you're barely holding on, it feels as though you're completely alone. You're not. Depression is a disease which isolates us, pushing us away from everything and everyone we love. It chills, freezing hearts one cut at a time. It makes it hard to remember that there's anything other than the cold, other than the loneliness. Take these words and hold them as tight as you can: There IS someone out there who cares, someone who'll listen without judgment, who'll love you, no matter what your flaws.

You are loved, don't forget that.

You are loved.

Love, Me

# 26

Take a breath, shake your limbs, say what you are feeling out loud, and listen to hear yourself. Your voice is a unique, precious expression of who you are and we need it in this world.

Kyle Keane

# 27

Dear Stranger,

I don't know you, and I know you might be tired of people who don't know you telling you how you should feel or act or think. I know I don't understand the intricacies of your feelings and troubles, and it would be rude of me to pretend I know what goes on in your head and life and suggest I have a magic solution. What I can tell you, however, is what has gone on in my head as a friend, acquaintance and stranger to people who are feeling similarly to you. There are so many things I wish I could have said to the people I have encountered in my life who have attempted to take their own lives, and I hope you will humor me and let me say a few of them to you.

Even though it sounds trite, I suppose the most important thing I can say is that people want to help. They want to help because they care about you, and want you to be happy. They might not know how to help, and they might not know how much help you need… if they even know you need help at all. You might not want to let people in. You might not want to burden people with your problems, or trust them with your troubles. But chances are that if you open up and share your struggles, people will respond with a sincere desire to help you. Some people may never understand, perhaps out of their own fear and insecurity with themselves, but so many more will be thrilled and honored to be trusted to help you deal with your pain. It won't be pity, it won't be a feeling of obligation, and though they might not have any easy answers, they will have a shoulder to cry on and a sympathetic ear. They will do their best to take you in when you need a refuge, be a support when you feel alone and afraid, and give you the love it may be hard for you to give yourself sometimes.

If you have been burned by trusting others in the past, it only means you need to cast your net wider, because people like us are out there, and we won't know how to help you (or even if you need help at all) unless you let us know. Most likely, you seem perfectly wonderful, happy and in control to most people around you, and few will recognize how much you are suffering inside. Many of us won't realize you are struggling unless you flat out tell us. Some of us might even realize it, but be too insecure and afraid and that we would fail you as a friend to reach out uninvited- we fear that we wouldn't know what to say to make you feel better, or what to do to fix the problems that are causing you pain. We are all insecure and afraid in our own ways, and hesitant to assume we can be of any use to you as a friend. But if you give us the chance to be there for you, we will do our best- because we will want to alleviate any aspect of your suffering that we can, even if all we can do is make sure you don't ever have to feel alone. I suppose that is the crux of this argument: you truly are not alone. There are so many out there who care about you and don't know how to best be there for you. Reach out, and don't stop reaching out. You will find us, and we will show you how much we care. You will never have to feel alone.

Yours, truly,

A Friend

# 28

Only those who have felt the coldness of life can truly appreciate the warmth of a hug.

It's only when you get as low as you can get that will you know what is really important. When the things you once took for granted are gone. When the things you need are the things that money can't buy. When the life you used to live is like a dream. Then you will see the kindness of a stranger, then you will value the loyalty of friend, then you will say I love you and mean it with all of your heart. Doesn't that person sound amazing? Wouldn't the world be a better place with that person in it? Well that person is you my friend, someone who has learnt the true value of the things in their life. The world deserves to be filled with people like that, with people like you.

You are already a survivor, you've made it this far. I want you to keep going. I want you to keep going and join the other survivors. We're all around you. You'll recognise us; you know what to look for. And when you find one, hug them; remind them that the world needs them too.

# 29

I think there is something you should know:  Things might not be happening how you planned… But you've made it through so far because you're so strong.


You are Loved

# 30

To be nobody but yourself in a world which is doing its best, night & day, to make you everybody else, means to fight the hardest battle which any human being can fight, and never stop fighting.

Do you keep wondering what you're really supposed to be spending your time doing? Join the club. All I know is that you have to be happy when you fall asleep.

Sometimes you have to face those people that you just don't think you can. Sometimes you have to face those moments that push you to be the person you are meant to be. Be brave my friend. I'm facing them right now. We can do this together!

All right, I'm not much for words of wisdom or pep talks. Are you searching for a friend, maybe you want an adventure. I don't know your story. Thousands of people are out there - you just have to start the story at the beginning. Someone will listen. Someone always listens eventually. I want to thank you, Anonymous - (If you're a guy, I'll call you Carter, if you're a woman, I'll call you Lilly - Please don't take any offense, I like these names, they make me feel like I'm talking to a friend, Anonymous.) Enough about you for a second. I am searching. We all are. I'm searching for that one great adventure, that moment where I can truly say that I've accomplished something. I want to learn French, I want to marry my current boyfriend, but above all, I want to be happy - not rich, not famous, happy. I have suffered with bipolar disorder Anonymous. If you don't know about it, it's very common. But it's terrible. I've wanted pain and sorrow before, and I've wanted to do terrible things. Depression is terrifying. I just want you to know that there is always someone there for you, whether you believe it or not, Anonymous. You are a beautiful human being. Good luck with your life.

# 32

Dear Stranger,

You're one in a million. One in Billions actually. That's probably hard for you sometimes, to step back and totally realize what a small part of the world you are.

It's okay. It's hard for me too. We get tangled in the moments and intricacies of our lives. It's ok, stranger. Take a step back and breathe. Breathe and feel the breath of the 7 billion people that surround you. Fell the pulse of the world as it turns.

Then, feel yourself and soul expand into the space you've at once created and discovered. Live in the big picture, if only for a moment, then dive back in stronger. And take on your own life with a greater understanding of the lives that go on around you.

Do this for me,

Because I love you stranger.

# 33

Hello Stranger,

Sometimes I feel like life gets too difficult to even go on. When I feel this way, I stop and realize I have two options. The first is to give up. Although this is the easiest option, giving up will leave exactly where you are, this sad, desolate, and defeated place. However, there is a second option and that is to keep going, to keeping pushing through even when you feel crushed by the weight of the world. Taking the second option takes more strength and courage then we think we have. It takes all of our energy, both physically and mentally to just keep trying. Eventually out efforts will repay us. We will be victorious. The battle it took to get there will only make the victory that much sweeter.

So whatever you are facing, whatever your demons are, keep going. It's worth it.

XOXO

A Stranger

# 34

To Whom it may concern

When I was a little girl I would say my prayer before I went to sleep,

Now I lay me down to sleep
I pray the lord my soul to keep
If I die before I wake
I pay the lord my soul to take
Please don't make me wake up

By the time I was 7 or 8 I gave up on any god as I woke up every morning and I had been praying for a long time.

By the time I was 11 I would run in front of cars in hopes of getting hit and killed. I started drinking and smoking when I was 12. Sex came with that and a very destructive life ensued. I won't go into details but I shouldn't be alive.

When I was 15 I had it figured out, I went to the beach and once everyone was gone I was going to swim as far as I could, knowing I would not make it back as I was not a strong swimmer. As I sat and waited a guy come up to me and started talking. After about 10 minutes he asked me if I wanted to go up north with him and his friends. I looked at him (he looked dangerous) and I said yes. So I was on my way up north with 3 guys I had no idea what they might do, but hopeful one of them would kill me.

18 months later I returned home with my 3 month old baby girl. A little person who needed me and loved me. My reason to live. I could have found many reasons without having a child. But I really needed her more then she needed me.

I now have 3 kids and sometimes I still entertain that thought. Things like "they'd be better off without me" or "my life really doesn't matter" but then I remind myself, I do matter and I do make a difference. Every smile I give to a stranger, every good deed has a ripple effect and it makes a BIG difference to those I will never meet or understand how much it meant to that person. Just as those who helped me will never know how much a difference they made to me.

I want to thank them all for the positive words, help when I didn't know they were helping and just being there at the right time with a smile.

THANK YOU!!!

Special thanks to the guy who took me back to my home until I knew what I wanted to do. He changed me most of all. I will forever be in his debt.

Just know you're not alone. People do care. You do make a difference even if you don't see it. It's like the ripples in the water when you throw a stone, you don't realize how far your small act of kindness goes. Accept help from others. By doing so you are helping them too.

Best quote from a movie "we except the love we think we deserve"

The Perks of being a Wallflower

Always know you deserve more then you let yourself have. Don't be afraid to have more love then you know what to do with. No one has ever died from an overdose of love.

Hugs from a friend who has worn a similar pair of shoes. You will make it. It is never too late to try on other shoes.

Thank you. Good luck

# 35

We haven't met yet but one day we will and everything will fall into place. One day, our two lost souls that have always been meant for each other will reunite and we will be one.

I image looking into your eyes, losing myself in the feeling of having you in my life. You might not believe me now but I know that magic is possible. Believe me, we will be magical!

There are days when I miss you badly and my whole body aches for your love. Yet you give me strength. I am secure in knowing that one day, we will be very happy together. Believe me, we will be crazy about each other!

Don't wait for me - we will find each other when the time is right. Live your life to the fullest and enjoy all the adventures you find along the way. Embrace every day of your life just for being alive and remember that you are never alone.

One day, I will love you with all my heart.

A stranger.

# 36

I hope you are having a lovely day and that this letter finds you well! I am having a wonderful day myself, especially because we are standing on the very beginning of fall! Do you love fall? I hope you do! I absolutely love it!

There's something magical about it, ya know? The air grows crisp and cool, the leaves change and fall, and of course I can't forget football. :) Do you like football? I'm a huge fan of it!

I hope you know how incredible you are! You are never alone. You are beautiful. You are valued. You are so important. And you are loved.

Happy September, my friend!

# 37

I hope this letter finds you well... I want you to know that you are special, and that you can do anything you set your mind to. It took me a great deal of trial and error to learn that for myself. For too long I allowed family, significant others, and "friends" to pull me down with negativity.

But you know what? We only have one change to be here - one life to live. So live. Live your life the way you want. - The way that fills your heart with love, joy, and pride. Know that there is someone who believes in you, who believes in your dreams and aspirations.

I wish you happiness, love, and I wish for you peace of mind. You are unique... (((Hugs))) Smile!

Love,

Me

# 38

Dear Perfect Stranger,

Today I dare you to smile. It doesn't matter why. Simply smile. It could be over something that's seemingly insignificant, like the sound of a soda can opening, or it could be over something a bit more meaningful like a loved one laughing. Whatever the reason, a smile will brighten your day... I promise. :)

If you can't seem to find something to smile over I will give you a very good reason. YOU ARE ALIVE! :)

You are alive. You are here... for a reason. So smile about it! So go forth and grin wider than the Cheshire Cat! :D

Have a wonderful day! Sincerely,

Just Another Stranger

"The proper order of things is often a mystery to me. You, too?" -Cheshire Cat

# 39

Dear Stranger,

There are so many people in this world who wake up with a frown on their face, perhaps it's because they've forgotten how to smile, and maybe one of those people is you.

"You will see the world for all that it is, and for all that it is not, what you should do, is choose to see the world the way you wish it to be, so that way every day will be a new adventure." - I wrote that myself. Wake up in the morning with a smile on your face, set your sights high, and make your dreams come true. Do what makes you happy and do a good deed. Knowing that you've made someone else's day just by leaving a little note, or helping someone across the street, it only takes a little to mean a whole lot.

Most importantly, never forget who you are, don't try to be anybody but yourself. You are not alone. There are so many people who shift and change. They work so hard to be what everyone else wants them to be. INDIVIDUAL. That's what you are. None of us are the same. Be a little weird, a little quirky. Put yourself before others, "what's best for myself?"

I care about you stranger, whether you're homeless, rich, living in a mansion, or poor living on welfare. There are too many people in this world to worry about which path of life they've come from. Here is a goal for you: Make a new friend today and show them who you really are.

- From a Stranger who cares :)

# 40

Dear Stranger,

What do I have to say that could brighten your day, make you feel empowered or make you reflect on the wonders of your life? Perhaps I can't. If I could maybe I would have done that for myself.

Nobody knows what is in my heart or my head. I let nobody in. Are you the same? Would we feel better if we were honest and open to others? Maybe you already are. If not shall we try? Shall we challenge ourselves to let others know how we feel even though they might reject us?

A song that always gets me thinking is Very Kind by Will Young.

"You got wings but you can't fly, you got so much pain inside."

"In your dreams you're so high. But you don't live that in your life."

How can we make ourselves fly in our waking moments? How can we believe in ourselves and not care what others think about us as long as we love ourselves? How can we search out opportunities to show our strengths and prove to ourselves our worthfullness?

I know dear stranger that you are a good, kind, wonderful person. That you have such a positive effect on the world and the people around you. Rejoice in this and know that you can fly just by being yourself. The world would be a sadder place without you in it.

Love always to you dear stranger, from a stranger who believes in you.

# 41

If ever we are in passing, I hope to look at you with soft sensitive eyes. I hope to gaze into your soul with a smiling heart that is filled with love for you, even if it's only for a split second. Knowing that we may never spot each other again, I give myself to you for the time that we do share. My whole being is yours, all of my attention and thought on you. But do not be frightened, for I will not pass judgment on your so called flaws and I will not discriminate against you for the skeletons in your closet. In this very instance, you can be yourself, and I will have witnessed one of the greatest masterpieces ever to be made. I will have seen you.

# 42

Dearest Stranger,

I am writing you this letter because I want you to know that you are loved beyond words. I want you to know that all these things that are causing you to be sad, worried or disappointed will not matter 10 years from now, so just hang in there.

Life is a win-win situation, even if it looks like we're losing. We'll actually win in the end. Our past mistakes will not define us and what we are going to be in the future, this is just a part of living. All the things and moments, whether they are good or bad, make us unique and special in a way. Do not ever compare yourself to someone else because all of us are different, thus all of us are special.

My dearest stranger, I want you to read this letter every time you are feeling sad, lost, disappointed, upset or insecure. I want you to feel strong and defy all the odds that you are facing. I wish for you to live ~ experience life. I wish you all the best my love. Keep smiling.

Love lots, Anonymous

# 43

Dearest Stranger,

Today did not start out well. I was upset when I went to bed last night and my anger followed me into the morning. That little voice that helps you make decisions was telling me that I was a bad person... ugly... unlovable... stupid...

I decided to stop for coffee on the way to work, and the most amazing thing happened: the woman at the window smiled at me. It was a brilliant, genuine smile. As a reflex, I smiled back... and I felt better. Not great... but better. The voice got quieter. My heart got lighter.

You never know how the tiniest of kind gestures can change someone's day.

This is me, sending a genuine smile to you.

I believe that you are a good person who is capable of good things. I believe that by being kind, you can make a difference in the world. I believe that if you do what you can with what you have, where you are, you will be a success.

Above all, I believe that you were born to be exactly who you re. Don't be afraid to let down your walls and be yourself. It's scary, but it's worth it.

Go read The Chronology of Water by Lidia Yuknavitch. Go listen to Why Should the Fire Die? by Nickel Creek. Go watch Rear Window. Surround yourself with the beauty of the world.

- And remember that you are part of what makes this world beautiful.

With the sincerest of smiles,

Anonymous

# 44

Dear Stranger,

I hope this letter reaches you when you're at high spirits and places. One of the most curious aspects that comes with writing a letter to a stranger is that it becomes a sort of reflection. The letter meant for a stranger is a truer reflection of the writer than a letter to a friend. Or perhaps I am looking too deep into things.

There's so much I can tell you, friend, about the world as I currently understand it and the way the waves crash like they do on perfect summer days like this one. I could tell you that, in accordance to String Theory and Everett's Many Worlds Interpretation, the universe splits itself at every event into each possible outcome, and each resulting universe is no less real than the rest. I could tell you about bonfires and late nights spent playing beer pong and sipping Bacardi and 7-Up. I can even tell you about how Fibonacci's number relates to LSD and the universe.

Instead I will tell you about myself, not because I think I'm such an interesting topic, but rather in an attempt to trap a piece of myself in these lines of 100% Post-Consumer Recycled Paper (true story.), and send it off to you, wherever you may be. Because a soul (or at least part of one) is worth more than all the two-cent advice I can spew out at you.

Recently I had my wisdom teeth removed. Now I have four wisdom holes. When I eat I can't tell what's stitches and what's cheek and what's food and what's swollen gums. I can't smoke hookah for a while, either, which is really such a shame because on summer nights I like nothing more than getting with friends and smoking hookah and maybe reading a book. On summer days I like nothing more than going to the beach.

The ocean is a glorious thing.

Once, with my friend Molly, I went to the beach. It was a cloudy day and nobody else was there. I've never seen anything more beautiful than the ocean. Part of me, if not most of me, wanted to run into the waves and past the waves and swim out as far and as deep as my body could handle, and then some, and become one with the ocean and the sweet earth.

Not suicide. Just unity. But I can't bring myself to give in to such romantic ideals.

I hope I'm not boring you, friend. Perhaps I should tell you more about myself, so you can put my words in context. David Bowie is the only god I want to worship. Osmosis Jones is my Spirit Animal. DMT is the only afterlife I want to believe in. I hope to glob that we live in an oscillating universe. The Big Rip would be a crying shame. But in all probability it's our fate. C'est la vie. Rein a faire.

If by now you haven't realized, I'm a huge science nerd which means I've somehow developed the sillier belief that it's possible. It's all just very silly.

Well, dear friend, I think now I really ought to get over myself and give you some advice. That's what these letters are for, are they not? To help you, my friend, to the best of my ability.

Because who wants another's soul, or a piece of it? What would you do with it? Hang it on the wall to look pretty, roll a joint with it, and wrap a present? In this day and age, another's soul (or a piece thereof) is probably the last thing you'd like to find in your mailbox. I'm sorry there's no gift receipt.

My first piece of advice: don't take anything I say seriously. I never do. Because I've never been able to take anything seriously in my entire life. My only flaw.

My second piece of advice manifests itself in the form of an anecdote:

*Brief disclaimer: if you happen to be of the religious sort, please don't think any less of me for fostering these beliefs. In fact, feel free to skip this second piece of advice entirely and go right on down to the third.

Once upon a time there was a young girl raised in a Christian household. She went to church every Sunday and prayed to god every night and did her very best not to sin. This little girl had scoliosis but decided not to seek medical attention because she prayed about it every night ~ God would provide.

The one day she was on the interwebs (a dangerous pastime indeed) and saw the immensity of the stars and galaxies and universe and came to the conclusion that any religion here on earth probably wasn't correct. She believed that the bible, if it ever contained the words of god, was lost in translation and human error, and that it was, at least now, more the word of man than anything. So it can be said that the young girl lost her faith in orthodox religion. She became atheist, and thought that anyone who still believed was simply ignorant and clinging to mythology.

But then she found out that one of her teachers, her role models, was extremely catholic. This confounded her. How could such a brilliant man believe in the god of an orthodox religion? She realized that religion has faith in a higher being whereas science has faith in mankind's logic and reason.

One day she was smoking hookah at a friend's house, petting a kitten, and watching Louie. On the T.V. screen a guy was about to use a glory hole labelled "heaven", and Louie asked him why he would do such a thing, to which the man replied, "why not?"

And the young girl realized that it was horrible to look down on anyone who believed in religion, that religion and science should grow symbiotically, and that with such a complex universe (and an even more complex multiverse), if there is a higher being afterall, He sure is great. As in very large and very capable. But she still suffers from scoliosis.

The moral of the story is that atheists and theists can coexist, science and religion both require faith, and medical needs require medical attention.

Advice #3 is simple: Traffic safety is not a joke.

4) All things in moderation. Even moderation.

5) Safety second.

Advice #6 is perhaps the most important. If you take anything away from this letter, my friend, remember this:

Fall in love at least once a day.

This is the trick to keeping the soul alive and nourished. Read a book. Climb a tree. Sing in the shower. Write a poem, even a lousy poem. Every day, find something beautiful and fall in love, and don't be afraid to remark, "if this isn't nice, I don't know what is." (Kurt Vonnegut Jr. said that)

My seventh piece of advice might sound counter-intuitive due to the monstrosity of the current school system, but here goes: math is a beautiful thing. Enjoy it.

It's universal and introduces some of the most abstract ideas I can think of. So even though the modern school system's hell bent on making the youth detest math, do yourself (and the world) a favor and look into it. Discover its beauty.

Look up a harmonograph and Fibonacci's sequence and the Thue-Morse Sequence and all the rest. It'll make you a worldlier person.

Advice #8 is easy: laugh as much as possible.

#9 is to sit up straight. Posture is important for first impressions, and first impressions are important to all the rest.

And finally #10: Be concerned for the ozone layer and the earth. Our actions will not only decide the fate of a country or a race, but for all life on earth.

Humans have all the potential in the world; we just have to stop using the power of the cerebral cortex for the goals of our reptilian brains. Stop backwards thinking.

And with that, my friend, dear stranger, I'm out. Thanks for listening.

# 45

Beloved Stranger.

I just love that word. Beloved. It sounds so poetic. I've always been fascinated by the English language. My own language is poetic in its own way, but with the English language I can play with the words in another way. Like beloved. We have our own version of that word, but it's not the same. Not at all.

Most people don't take time to reflect on things. But my dear stranger, somehow I imagine you do. I imagine that you think a lot. I know I do. And maybe I'm just hoping for someone else to do it too.

Life is an amazing thing. It's a movie and a book, a never ending story about our lives. We're all the main character in our own story, but sometimes we forget that fact. We are so busy fulfilling the part of being the best friend to someone else's story that we forget to be the main character in our own.

My dearest stranger, I want to remind you that you are the main character in your own story. That you are amazing and deserve the best, no matter what anyone else tells you. You are strong and unique, no one can ever replace you, and I admire you greatly. Make sure you make this year your best year ever. Do the crazy things you've dreamt of doing but never really dared to. Dance in the rain, laugh a lot and enjoy life.

And I will try to do the same. We deserve this, my dear stranger. Let's make this our year. No self-inflicted restrictions, no what ifs, no second guessing ourselves. We are amazing, and we can do anything we set our minds to. So let's start now.

I wish you all the best.

# 46

Today would have been my Dad's 54th birthday. The last one he was alive to celebrate was his 51st, at which point he had a mental age of about 12. I don't mean he was in touch with his inner child so much as he had spent the last nine months aging backwards at an accelerating pace from a brain tumor. We didn't yet have to spoon-feed him, but we sure couldn't let him out on his own, either. He loved his birthday pie, which was filled with strawberries and extra love. But maybe in this state he was privy to something we weren't, maybe was more in touch with his inner child than I give him credit for. He spent the last months of his life laughing, loving, living and not just surviving. When people brought gifts or hugs, he accepted gratefully without any of the "Oh-no-you-shouldn't have" bullshit adults have been trained into. He took naps and went potty as he pleased. The part of his brain responsible for anxiety was largely collateral damage now, and frankly he was better for it until the reason killed him.

I'm writing you this letter because I wanted to share a story with a stranger, but you're receiving it for a different reason. You're receiving it because you deserve a bright spot in your day. I don't know why, but you do. Take a moment and consider what you've done or who you've been that deserves an award that no one has recognized you for. Here is your award for you keep with you. I hope it reminds you that you are special for the you that you bring to the world.

But the award comes with one price. Pass on an act of kindness. It can be for a stranger, a friend, or a familiar stranger. It can be another letter or a quarter in someone's parking meter. Whatever it is, I hope it negates a little piece of anxiety in your brain.

Who I Am Makes A Difference

I don't know a lot, but I do know you're better than you think you are. I know you struggle with life in some way, and I want you to know that I do too.

I don't know a lot, but I know I'm a paradox. I want to be happy, but I'm complacent in my sadness. I'm lazy, yet ambitious. I don't like myself, but I'm in love with who I am. I feign confidence, yet I breathe insecurities. I crave attention, though I reject it when it comes my direction. I know that I am a conflicted contradiction. If I can't figure myself out, there's no way anyone else has.

When you are sure you're worthless and nothing, look again for the beauty and grace I know is there. If you can't find it, look again. Confidence is not self-satisfaction; it's the faith one has to find their light in the darkness of the world.

Keep looking

I am sending you today something special. It is called INSPIRATION. I want you to be inspired by no one other than yourself. True, we have a lot of people we can get inspiration from. But nevertheless we must find inspiration within ourselves. I have looked at myself and wondered who really inspires me. As a child it was my mother father and anyone else who I could look up to. I guess as children it is easy to find a mentor or someone to look up to. But as you grow older you really wonder is the inspiration you get from outsiders the true inspiration. Does it really motivate me to excel in the things I truly want to excel. Or should I motivate myself to find that deep sense of inspiration solely within me. These are questions I have always asked myself. True, I have always wanted to be the next most compassionate person. And there are a lot of folks who you can draw your inspiration to be compassionate. But at the end of the day I am not sure you can achieve anything without lifting yourself up to be what you really want to be.

So as I am writing to you, I wonder if you have achieved everything you wanted and are content with life or you are just one of those that is still looking out for the next power ball lottery to be won. No matter what stage you are in your life you still need something more, something to make you excited every morning-something to jump out of bed and say- I am really looking forward to it. That is why I am saying life needs to be inspired all the time- by people around you but most importantly by you.

I hope after reading this letter you will find something that you will do today and tonight as you go to bed you will say- Yes, this letter inspired me to do this! Trust me if you do I will feel it all - no matter where you are. I will smile when you smile and somewhere in the universe we will be bound by a common thread to this thought.

Peace and get inspired now!

MD

## 49

This is harder than I expected. I guess I'll start by saying that I love to stand in the pouring rain. There's something so renewing about it. I am forever interested in reinventing myself. I believe that people are never done growing. Just as soon as you've learned something about yourself, there is always something else to keep searching for. I used to think that love could not be real. How could someone love you if you're never done finding out who you are? But love is kind. It allows someone to not only love who you are now, but also who you will be in the future. Accept those around you that you love. If you don't, you will never be able to accept yourself, or who you will become. I'd like to conclude by leaving an Emerson quote.

"What lies behind us and what lies before us are tiny matters compared to what lies within us."

# 50

Dear Stranger,

You. Are. Beautiful. Inside and out. I want to tell you how much you are appreciated. Without you, this world would not be quite the same. If it weren't for you, I probably would not be awake right now. I wouldn't be as happy without you - knowing that this letter will never touch your hands the way they are touching it now. Beautiful, dear, admirable stranger - Do me a favor. Look around you. Look up. Look down. Look at yourself. Deep into yourself. Are you happy? Are you happy as you could be? Should be? What would make you happier, just what would make you smile? One hour ago, 5 minutes ago, until the VERY last second you opened this letter, you didn't know I existed. But now stranger, we will forever be connected in a sense of anonymity! We're friends! I want the best for you. I want you to live a remarkable, joyous life. I wish you only good things, and long-lasting health, and wisdom and sensibility. Because that is what a friend does for another. Stranger, friend, brand new acquaintance-

I CHALLENGE you:

To try something different each and every day of your life. To do what makes you happy. To live without regrets. To make new friends and meet different people! To breathe and feel at peace. To ACCEPT YOURSELF for who you are.

Life is already difficult. Why make it any harder?

I will never forget you. You are loved.

(heart) Your Stranger

# Conclusion

I hope that this book has done what it was meant to do – inspire you. I know that it is short. Yes, there are only 50 letters in here, but there are so many other people who love you. If you are in a situation in which you don't feel loved, leave. Go somewhere new with new people and I promise that you will be loved. Wherever you go and whatever you do, take this book with you. We are 50 people who have your back. We are 50 people who will stand beside you. We are 50 people who love and accept you. If (or when) you feel like you have finished needing this book, please pass it on. Thank you for being you.

Easy Publishing Company